[PRECEDING PAGE]
In this scene, Indy has emptied the pellets from shot-gun shells and used them to locate a magnetic field that holds a clue. When he tosses them up, they fly toward the field, leading him to the top of a stack of crates. Director of photography Janusz Kaminski did a fabulous job here with the smoke and backlight. Life is a lot easier for a still photographer when you have a talented cinematographer to work with. Janusz's way of lighting always gives me plenty of leeway to use my own angles or to adopt those of the film camera.

[RIGHT]
Steven and Shia with the toys of men and boys—the iPhone and the yo-yo. It's worth noting that the iPhone debuted worldwide during the production of *IJ4*. You'll spot them periodically throughout the book.

[FOLLOWING PAGE]
Harrison Ford's shadow. Deming, New Mexico

INSIGHT EDITIONS

17 Paul Drive : San Rafael : CA : 94903
www.insighteditions.com
phone 415.526.1370 : fax 415.526.1394

Library of Congress Cataloging-in-Publication Data available.

ISBN-13: 978-1-933784-64-9

ROOTS of PEACE   REPLANTED PAPER

Palace Press International, in association with Roots of Peace, will plant two trees for each tree used in the manufacturing of this book. Roots of Peace is an internationally renowned humanitarian organization dedicated to eradicating land mines worldwide and converting war-torn lands into productive farms and wildlife habitats. Together, we will plant two million fruit and nut trees in Afghanistan and provide farmers there with the skills and support necessary for sustainable land use.

10 9 8 7 6 5 4 3 2 1

Printed in China by Palace Press International

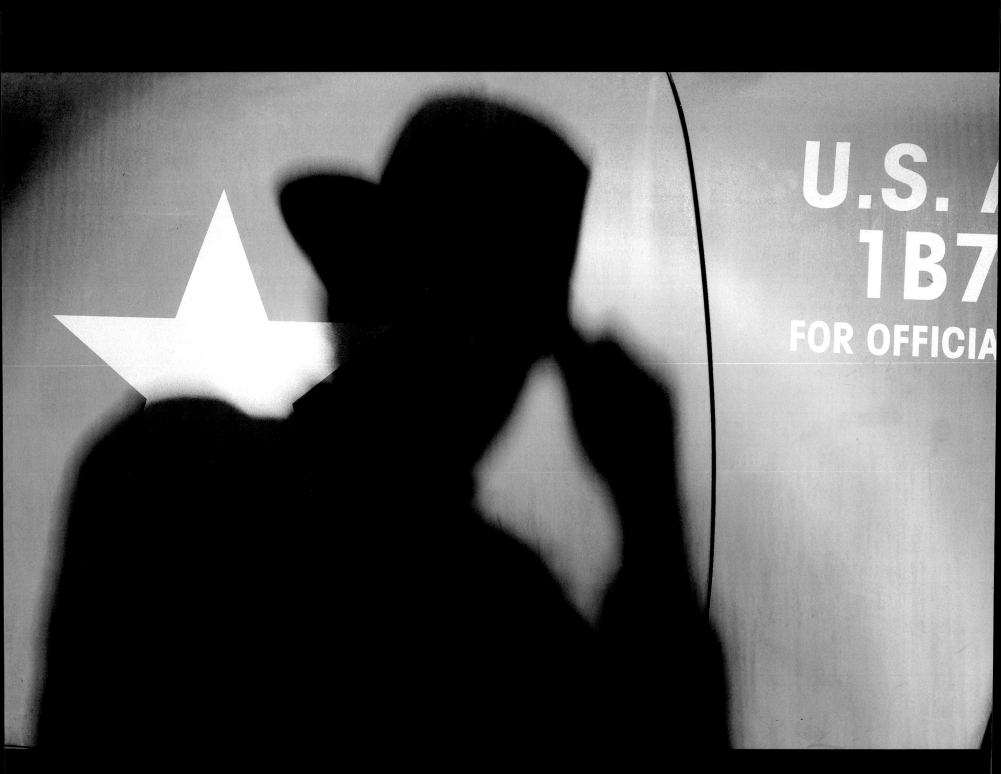

A PHOTOGRAPHIC JOURNAL

BY DAVID JAMES

INSIGHT EDITIONS

San Rafael, California

CONTENTS

PREFACE

BY STEVEN SPIELBERG

When thinking of the importance and power of on-set unit photography, I always remember the classic François Truffaut film *Day for Night.* In addition to making this unforgettable picture, Truffaut also acted in it, playing a director obsessed with movies who has recurring dreams of himself, as a kid, in which he steals from a movie theater—not the one-sheet poster, not the print of the film—but the lobby cards (in other words, the *stills*) of *Citizen Kane.* Whether in the lobby of a movie theater or in a magazine—or on the Internet—audiences make first contact with our movies through the photographs taken on set during production. Unit photography helps us introduce our films to audiences and, later, after they've watched the movie, seeing the photograph of a scene will hopefully deepen their appreciation of a movie moment. Undoubtedly, still photography is an art. It is also a necessity. And marrying both is a skill that David James has mastered for many years.

David became a member of our on-set family when he joined the crew of *Schindler's List* in 1993. Since then, he has shot memorable stills for several of my films—including *Saving Private Ryan* and, more recently, *Indiana Jones and the Kingdom of the Crystal Skull*—and for one mini-series I produced, *Band of Brothers.* As I write these lines, he is coping with tropical heat, explosions, and the other trials of a demanding eight-month shoot in Australia for *The Pacific*—our follow-up to *Band of Brothers.*

I think of the still photographer as a species of photojournalist: He or she documents what happens on a movie set, capturing our behind-the-scenes journey as well as the film's narrative. Each frozen moment tells a story, so a book such as this one provides a priceless record of what went into a film's creation. On this documentary level, David is the consummate professional; he always knows where to place himself to take maximum advantage of the production design, the lighting, and the performances in a given setup. But there's more to his craft. Looking at still images is by nature a very different experience from seeing a film on the screen—so it's vital that the photographer work closely with the director to understand his intentions in each shot and to try to capture the film's overall look and tone. Some unit photographers come closer than others, yet no one is better at this than David. His choices are inspiring and his images are always perfect companions to my films.

On *Crystal Skull,* with the collaboration of my trusted director of photography Janusz Kaminski, I was determined to honor the visual legacy of the first three films: strong colors; high-key lighting; and breathtaking, elaborate physical sets, designed in this case by production designer Guy Hendrix Dyas. The production was very much in the tradition of old-fashioned filmmaking, where the actors were playing against a three-dimensional reality rather than in front of a bluescreen, which, to my regret, is a luxury and a rarity today. Guy and his team created visual environments of incredible richness and complexity; but ironically these often go by very quickly on the motion-picture screen. Consequently, David's stills played a critical role in documenting the fruit of all this collective labor; his stills showcase and pay tribute to the amazing, yet ephemeral work that went into the design of the film.

Besides capturing "freeze-frames" of the action, emotion, and excitement from the film, David has also caught, I think, the relaxed yet energized mood of our close-knit cast and crew during our eighty-day shoot. The spirit that existed on the set is reflected in David's photography, so as I look at the book it feels like going through the pages of a family album. These images will always bring back for me the pleasures of working on the fourth *Indy* film. It was a special experience for me and for my wonderful collaborators both in front of and behind the camera—one that gave us the opportunity to practice old-school, set-based filmcraft. We all brought our best to the effort, which I think will be evident to anyone who looks at David's pictures. Beyond my own personal and emotional connection to this journal, what David has compiled is a gift not only to fans of *Indiana Jones* but also to those who appreciate great photography.

[PREVIOUS PAGE]
Harrison Ford and Shia LaBeouf. New Haven, Connecticut.

[LEFT]
Steven Spielberg. New Haven, Connecticut.

FOREWORD

BY HARRISON FORD

I first met David James when we worked together on Sydney Pollack's 1999 film, *Random Hearts*. David was there, getting it all, and always—and this distinguishes him from some others I've worked with—very discreet. He never intrudes on an actor or a director's work. He always picks an interesting angle from which to shoot. Quietly squeezing into the right position at just the right moment, he got great shots. I'd never notice him when the cameras were rolling. I'm not a "get out of my eye-line" kind of guy, but if I were, David would be my man. The other thing I remember is his remarkable gift for photographing people off-camera in ways that capture the individuals and their relationships—both working and personal.

Besides his day-to-day duties on the set on *Indiana Jones and the Kindom of the Crystal Skull*, David was given the responsibility for "special photography." David asked me to help him get shots featuring the whip; unfortunately he got a bit too close—the whip wrapped around his wrist. That's dedication.

Crystal Skull was a reunion of sorts, with Steven, George, Frank, Kathy, Karen, and many others from the first three films. It was, as well, a chance to meet many new, very talented members of the cast and crew. I was delighted to be reunited with David. The quality of David's work is very high—as this photographic journal illustrates—and I think he's a terrific guy. I look forward to working on future projects with him.

[LEFT]
Steven Spielberg and Harrison Ford. Paramount Studios back lot, Los Angeles, California.

[RIGHT]
Harrison Ford. Las Cruces, New Mexico.

INTRODUCTION

BY DAVID JAMES

It was a cool summer night in the southern New Mexico desert, and the *Genre* crew was shooting an action scene. ("Genre" was the production code name for the new *Indiana Jones* movie, an attempt to maintain a low-key atmosphere around one of the most anticipated shoots in decades.) This was the sixth day of the shoot, and director Steven Spielberg typically had everything running like clockwork. We were out in the low hills around Las Cruces, New Mexico, and the setup was for the final moments in one of Indy's patented escapes. He's been battling Soviet bad guys inside the top-secret Hangar 51, and is hurtled into the desert at high speed on a 1950s "rocket sled."

I was on hand to shoot stills. Day or night, I was always on the set, as I never knew when the chance would come for a memorable shot. It was a promising setup: the landscape was dramatic; the special effects team was making smoke; our director of photography, Janusz Kaminski, had backlit the scene with a large 20-kilowatt light. As Harrison Ford–Indiana Jones for all time–ran up into the hills pursued by Russians, I positioned myself slightly off to one side, in a spot that placed Harrison in silhouette against the light cast through smoke and dust. I took a couple of test shots.

Shooting digitally, you can see right away if something has promise. I could tell this was a great opportunity and went over to show Steven–who appreciates the role that stills play in a production and always takes the time to review them with me when I have something that needs his attention. He immediately became excited about the image he saw on my camera, and actually stopped the line-up for a few minutes so I could take another shot before they moved on. (Once the line-up is done, the lighting changes; then the moment and opportunity are lost.) The few minutes' grace allowed me to capture an image that became an early teaser poster for the film that was given away at Comic Con 2007 in San Diego.

Everything that is so rewarding about working on a Steven Spielberg picture is embodied in this brief episode: the professionalism, the efficient use of time, Steven's pleasure in and attention to every aspect of filmcraft, his vision, and especially his willingness to support the stills effort–something that's rare among filmmakers in these days of time constraints.

When I was ten years old, growing up in England, MGM came to my village to shoot scenes for a movie outside my school. From that moment, I knew I wanted to be a stills photographer, and my life doing this work has been a series of great and magical adventures. Perhaps not quite like Indiana Jones, but more than exciting enough for me. Over the years the magic has never worn off; I still feel the excitement when I walk onto a set or into a studio.

After I moved from London to Hollywood, one of the most important events in my career took place in 1992, when my history with Steven began. I had heard through the industry grapevine that he would be shooting the Holocaust film *Schindler's List* mostly on location in Poland … and in black-and-white. As an artistic opportunity, this was every photographer's dream. I immediately delivered a portfolio to Steven's office at Amblin Entertainment. A few days later, to my great excitement and joy, I learned that I'd been awarded the job–although I didn't actually meet Steven until we were on location in Poland.

The night before shooting began, at a party for cast and crew, I introduced myself to him and asked, "What do you want to see from me?" To which he replied: "I only want to see what you want to show me. When I walk around a set, I'm followed by dozens of people; there are endless distractions. You walk around by yourself and see things that I don't–new angles, new possibilities. I want to see *that*." This was the best thing I could have heard.

This conversation has been the basis for all our work together since: on *Schindler's List*, on *The Lost World: Jurassic Park, Saving Private Ryan, Artificial Intelligence: AI, Minority Report,* the *Band of Brothers* TV miniseries, and now on *Indiana Jones and the Kingdom of the Crystal Skull.* (Our rapport continues on my current project: an eight-month shoot in Australia for *The Pacific*, another World War II miniseries and a counterpart to *Band of Brothers*.)

From the very first, we have enjoyed an excellent relationship and I have presented Steven with only my choices among the photos I've taken on any given day. I make proof sheets with four images to a page. Steven generally manages to look at these during lunchtimes, checking off his favorites and lining through any images he doesn't like (the "kills"). Then I go through the sheets, delete the kills, number the remaining ones, and send them off to the production company or the studio: in the case of *Indy IV*, to Lucasfilm. I also produce selected prints in a 16-by-12-inch format for Steven and the producers, for their reference and discussion.

There have been so many highlights in our collaboration. For example, one morning on the *Saving Private Ryan* set, I was on the beach when Steven arrived, looking for camera setups for the next scene. He called me over and asked to see what I had already shot. I brought him slides and a loupe, and from this viewing he took ideas for his next shot. It is remarkable: Whenever I say to Steven, "Take a look at this," he always finds the time to do it.

Crystal Skull was my first chance to be a part of the *Indiana Jones* experience. I'd read the advance press reports and was tremendously excited when I heard from producer Kathleen Kennedy in January 2006 that it would be going forward. I kept my calendar clear for this one!

Some of the featured cast members were new to me, though I knew Shia LaBeouf from the 2005 film *Constantine* and had worked with Harrison Ford on *Random Hearts*. I knew I could look forward to consummate professionalism and congenial cooperation from both. And I looked forward to experiencing once again the unique atmosphere of a Spielberg production as a member of Steven's shooting "family."

Even knowing what to expect, I was still struck by the level of comfort and happiness in the cast and crew that gathered in New Mexico in June 2007. Steven's unit is like an extended family: he works with so many of his team year after year—the level of trust is very high. Steven, George Lucas, and Harrison are themselves like a band of brothers; I think it is apparent in my photographs of them.

Steven's sets are also literally family affairs in that he makes all cast and crew family members welcome. His wife, Kate Capshaw, spent time on the set, along with several of their children. Their son Theo was an assistant director. Daughter Sasha had a cameo role, and daughter Jessica had her first child—Steven's first grandchild—during the filming. When Jessica visited the Marshall College set in Connecticut, she was visibly pregnant. On her return visit for the wedding scene at the end of filming, she arrived with a brand-new son in her arms. My wife and daughters, too, spent time with us on different locations, as did many family members of cast and crew.

On Steven's sets the atmosphere is always full of energy and good humor. Things move fast: the man is a dynamo and the crew follows in his wake. No two days are the same. There is never a chance to be bored, because there is always something going on—if I were to turn my back for ten minutes I would surely miss photo opportunities.

One of Steven's most important goals on this film was to recapture a sense of traditional moviemaking, shooting extended action sequences on huge, elaborate physical sets. The *Indy* series was based on the cliffhanger movie serials of an earlier age, and he has always tried to keep that freewheeling spirit, while surrounding the action with the best visual environments today's film industry can conjure up. The artists responsible for this on *Indy IV*–chief among them being Oscar®-winning DP Janusz Kaminski, a longtime collaborator with Steven, and production designer Guy Hendrix Dyas–are absolutely the best in the business. To shoot stills on the sets they designed, created, and lit was both a privilege and its own reward on every day of filming.

On a typical day I would arrive on the set early to get a feel for the day's work ahead. When possible I would watch the scene line-up (where the scene and camera positions are blocked out) to get an idea of what I was going to shoot. How much I shot on any given day totally depended on the scene: if it was two people sitting at a table talking, my shots would be minimal. However, if it was a battle or action scene I might shoot two hundred or more images, making the editing time longer but considerably more fun. On some productions (as with my current assignment on *The Pacific*), I may shoot stills for two different units, though on *Crystal Skull* the second unit was frequently working on stunts in a different location. All told, for *Crystal Skull* I shot 11,333 images, after editing.

Steven was his usual collaborative and involved self on this film. Normally I would find ways to take my pictures while he was shooting with the film cameras. If I am trying to catch action, I can usually find my own angles–it's not necessary to be right next to the camera, especially on exterior locations where there is plenty of natural light available. If I saw something I really wanted–something that was important to photograph from the same angle Steven took–he would often take time to repeat the shot with me in the place of the film camera.

Occasionally I would ask for a special setup with the actors–for example, with the heroes inside a cave on the Akator set, I found an angle and positioned the actors for my still. Such setups are sometimes the only way to get a great still, because moments on a set go by so fast. When they are over, that's it–opportunity gone.

Harrison, Cate Blanchett, Ray Winstone (Mac), Karen Allen, and Shia … I couldn't have wished for a better group. When we were shooting interiors in Los Angeles, I had a stills studio set up in one corner of a big soundstage at Downey. Part of my job is to take posed portraits for publicity and advertising art, but rarely is time dedicated just for this. On days when I thought we had opportunities to catch the actors between takes on the studio sets, I would bring assistants in, request an actor for a few moments, and rush them to my studio.

The company provided me with a trailer office to work in, sharing space with the publicity department. Because it was always a hive of industry in there, I tended to do my solitary work of editing and correcting images either very early in the morning or late in the evening, after shooting was done and everyone had gone home. Often I'll download images to the computer in the evening, then arrive before shooting the next morning, when it's quiet, and edit then. I prefer to do this kind of work alone, with low light and classical music playing. I find it hard to edit with people looking over my shoulder—they tend to want to know why I am selecting one shot over another, and this disturbs my concentration. I edit whenever I have the opportunity: sometimes if there is a long setup going on I'll head for the trailer or office. This quiet time is also when I work on images I have pre-selected as my "photographer's choices."

I do look forward to my editing time, but my work is rarely a solo act. Shooting stills for movies, you're a reportage photographer one minute, a portraitist the next, or a design photographer. Sometimes it seems like combat photography. In any case it's hugely collaborative—each image the result of your own thinking plus your reliance on others such as the director, production designer, costume designer, DP, art department, hair and makeup crews, grips, and electricians. It is not just my photograph; everyone has played a part in it.

Ultimately still photographs must reflect the movie, otherwise you haven't done your job. The essential goal is to get audiences excited about seeing the movie—to show the public what this amazing array of talent has created for them. That said, I always have my personal favorite images from any shoot, and this time I have had the good fortune to assemble my own book of those images.

The images you'll see here also reflect the varied assignments of the stills photographer: documenting the making of the movie with glimpses behind the scenes; capturing "in world" moments from the film, shot from similar angles to what the movie camera shows; taking evocative portraits of the cast members; as well as trying to capture moments that simply lend themselves to good photography. Due to the variety of shots that come out of these assignments, grouping the photographs together produces a number of organizational challenges. One approach would have been a straight "production diary," tracking the film shoot day by day. I thought about this way of chronicling the project and my experience, but concluded that it would produce a sometimes confusing experience for the reader—and one that didn't necessarily provide room for the best photographs. Because nearly all movies today are shot out of order, this would mean a lot of jumping around in the film story depending on what was shot where and when—on location or in the studio.

I instead chose to follow a rough chronology of the production, grouping photos according to the different locations where we shot the film. Within these general sections, I took some liberty in sequencing the photos, sometimes following the story of the film to make the experience as manageable as possible for readers so they could see how the behind-the-scenes photos work to illuminate the more "in world" shots I took, as well as relate my photos more directly to their memory of the film.

On occasion, I also did some more substantial re-ordering, including studio shots from later in the production with location shots that were captured well before, particularly for the early sections of the book. In the case of this film though, the production chronology roughly followed the film's narrative course. We actually began on location in the desert, where the crew shot what would become the very first scenes in the film and continued on from there. But those early scenes in the movie also include a lot of studio work that was done much later on. Whenever I've mixed the sequencing of images so that they strays this far from the production chronology in the galleries I've assembled, I've tried to indicate this so that my departures don't offer a false impression of how the movie was put together and so that readers who really are after a production diary aren't disappointed.

I hope you enjoy my collection of photographs from the making of *Indiana Jones and the Kingdom of the Crystal Skull*—as a record of this fantastically entertaining film, of the work that went into the project, and in their own right.

1

CONVOY TO HANGAR 51

Ghost Ranch and Deming, New Mexico; Downey Studios soundstage

Day 1 minus 3. A few days before the shoot began, I flew with my equipment from LAX to Albuquerque, to get set up and scout the first location while things were still relatively quiet. Arriving on each new set meant many hours of work: unpacking cameras and accessories, computer, monitors, printers, and drives. It was the middle of June, unbelievably hot, dry, and dusty in the New Mexico desert—hard on the equipment and hard on us.

Shooting was to start on Monday the 18th of June, 2007. On Saturday I made a foray out to Ghost Ranch, a 21,000-acre private reserve in northern New Mexico. Here the film's opening scene would be shot: a disguised convoy of Soviet personnel carriers crossing the desert on its way to the infamous Hangar 51. Crew and cast were lodged at various inns in Santa Fe and the nearby village of Abiquiu. Ghost Ranch is a starkly beautiful high-desert landscape, a broad river valley framed by stunning mountains and brilliantly colored rock formations. It was Georgia O'Keeffe's favorite place to paint, and the locations department knew

[RIGHT]
On the road. Ghost Ranch, New Mexico.

Steven would love it. That Saturday, I saw the road that locations manager Mike Fantasia had arranged to have paved for the filming, which was then "aged" by production designer Guy Hendrix Dyas and his team. I took some shots of the convoy on test runs.

It's pretty rare that the first day of filming records the actual opening scene of a movie—as if anything more were needed to make June 18, 2007, a special day. It began with a brief ceremonial moment to celebrate, at last, the launch of the new *Indiana Jones* movie after so many years in development. Steven welcomed everyone and lifted a glass of champagne to toast George Lucas, the crew, and the production. Then we all began our work.

A nice, throwaway moment in that first sequence is when the Soviet convoy is passed on the road by a quartet of 1950s teenagers racing in a '32 Ford roadster hotrod—very similar to the cars in George Lucas's *American Graffiti*. George is still crazy about fifties culture, so it was a little homage. Besides the expected shots of the convoy from various distances and angles, I had the opportunity to shoot George and Steven together in the roadster, grinning madly—a great moment.

On the afternoon of Day 2, we packed up the show and drove six hours south to a desert town less than fifty miles from the Mexican border. Deming, its little airport, and nearby Las Cruces would be shooting locations for the next six days; the crew HQ was Corralitos Ranch. At the airport, Mike had found an old, period-correct hangar to stand in for Hangar 51, and

in Las Cruces, about an hour's drive away, the art department built a set of gates where the Russians surprise the American guards and take control.

On Day 3, Harrison Ford arrived and did his first scene, when the Soviets pull Indy out of the trunk of a car. (They've kidnapped him.) Now it felt like an *Indiana Jones* movie. Cate Blanchett had just joined the shoot as well, and she was in character as the scary Irina Spalko from the moment she stepped on the set. Soon the action moves inside the hangar, with the first of several trademark scenes of Indy escaping and being pursued by the Russians … but shooting those interiors would have to wait for more than a month, until we moved onto soundstages around Los Angeles.

There are lots of clever nods to the earlier *Indy* films in *Crystal Skull*. Hangar 51, for instance, turns out to be the place where the Ark of the Covenant was entombed at the end of *Raiders of the Lost Ark*. Guy sent me some notes about the hangar set: "In terms of design, re-creating the top-secret storage hangar was all about turning the fantastic matte painting used in the first film into a real set. The matte painting showed an interior so vast that it was near-impossible to achieve the required scale in one space. So we used two different locations to create the illusion of one large warehouse."

As for what happens inside the hangar, I'll let the photos tell the story.

[PRECEDING LEFT-HAND PAGE]
Harrison Ford. Las Cruces, New Mexico.

[PRECEDING RIGHT-HAND PAGE]
It's a tradition with Steven that we all gather on the first day of shooting for a few words of welcome and a glass of champagne (I always have mine after the event as does the EPK–Electronic Press Kit–crew, since we're typically too busy shooting). Here Steven and George toast the success of the fourth *Indy* movie, eighteen years after *Indiana Jones and the Last Crusade*.

[ABOVE]
Steven asked me to shoot this picture of him and George wearing legionnaire caps. There is a parallel photograph from the set of the first *Indy* movie, also showing them both wearing the same style of hat.

[LEFT]
Laying a tarmac road on Ghost Ranch: $160,000.
1930s Ford roadster: $30,000.
Friendship and collaboration: Priceless.

It was a hot and dusty day. We arrived at the location at 7:00 A.M., giving me just enough time to set up my office and reacquaint myself with the crew. Steven is very loyal to his crews and they to him. Although faces change over the years, there is still a nucleus of the same people who began working with Steven on *Schindler's List* back in 1992.

Our first shots [LEFT] were of a convoy of military trucks manned by Soviets disguised as American soldiers. Our construction crew, whose members can turn their hands to any task, had built a tarmac road across the location. The convoy was to drive the length of the road, and then a group of kids in a roadster would drive up and race them for fun. The camera vehicle used for this shot was a Mercedes rigged with a boom arm. Designed for just such activities (every grown-up boy would love one–and, yes, I am one), this vehicle is capable of high speeds and maneuverability even when weighed down with a crane.

Steven [ABOVE] has no problem being photographed, but I am always respectful of the fact that he is working. At some moments when he is preparing a setup, though, I'm able to get right in front of him and shoot. When I do this, I can see the shot he's preparing, get in there, shoot it as well, and quickly get out. I love this shot–I used a fairly long lens to keep the background soft, and to avoid getting right in his face.

[PRECEDING LEFT-HAND PAGE, TOP]
The working space inside the Mercedes camera vehicle was very limited so I had to find other ways to get my shots. I loved photographing the rig, but I also needed to have some coverage of the scene. Here I positioned myself in the back using one of the soldiers for framing and in such a way that I couldn't see inside the army truck. This was one of those occasions when I got really excited about the image I caught. I showed it to Steven and he set up another shot from the same angle.

[PRECEEDING LEFT-HAND PAGE, BOTTOM]
Seven Spielberg and George Lucas. Ghost Ranch, New Mexico.

[PRECEEDING RIGHT-HAND PAGE]
Except for the Mercedes camera vehicle, this shot could be a classic image—a 1932 roadster cruising down the highway. Black umbrellas protect the actors from the desert sun.

[ABOVE]
I photographed Steven in front of the military compound gates on a very hot day at Las Cruces, Mexico. I couldn't resist getting him to pose in his Tin-Tin T-shirt because an upcoming project for him is to adapt the legendary comic albums by Hergé for the screen.

RESTRICTED AREA

WHILE ON THIS INSTALLATION
ALL PERSONNEL AND THE PROPERTY UNDER THEIR CONTROL
ARE SUBJECT TO SEARCH

USE OF DEADLY FORCE AUTHORIZED

SEC. 21 INTERNAL SECURITY ACT OF 1950

Gaffer David Devlin sets up a lamp for a shot. The cover helps keep the lamp cool in the intense heat. On location in the desert, lamps can easily become too hot. When they do, they automatically shut down–not good when you're trying to keep on schedule.

[RIGHT]
Key grip Jim Kwiatkowski steadies an extended crane arm for a shot. The crane is so finely balanced at this length the slightest wind becomes a problem.

[RIGHT]
When you're working long hours, a long way from home, you take any quiet moment you can to make a phone call to friends and family. I watched gaffer Devlin walk around for a while looking for one of those few magical spots in the desert where we could get reception. Finally, he found one.

[RIGHT]
The creative side of camera gripping comes into play when you need a shot that includes a mirror reflection. The camera head rests on a rig that is operated remotely; working at a distance, it takes a lot of skill to get this type of shot just right.

[MIDDLE]
Dovchenko and the other Soviets, posing as U.S. troops approach the guard gate. They then take the guards by surprise and gain entry to the airfield and hangar. I had to pose this group to obtain the right impact—it was one of those moments where I had to position myself right where the film camera had been.

[BOTTOM]
The reflection in the hubcap is of me shooting Steven. I'm always looking for a different view. That's part of the fun of being a photographer—keeping your eyes open and keeping close to what's happening. Here Steven and the team look at an angle that resulted in a complicated tracking shot. But when you see it on film, it flows so smoothly that you hardly notice.

[LEFT]
Igor Jijikine, who plays Dov, loves to be photographed and I loved photographing him. At one time he performed with Cirque du Soleil. It's easy to see that he's used to reaching the back of the theater with his facial expressions—they're quite extreme at times.

[ABOVE]

Getting George, Steven, and Harrison together at some point was a must. I wrangled all three for this shot, which only took a few minutes. It's a historic image in that it's Harrison's first day and also the first setup of the movie. He and Steven fell into gear as if no time had passed since they last worked together.

This scene [RIGHT] was shot at Deming, New Mexico, in searing temperatures; we were all very happy to be working in the shade of the hangar. The scene starts with Indy and Mac (Ray Winstone) in the trunk of the car, which must have been even hotter than it was outside. Acting isn't always a romantic illusion.

Makeup artist Bill Corso and hair stylist Karen Myers (Harrison's support team) apply sweat to Indy's face. Despite the ambient heat from the lighting and the real perspiration it causes, it's necessary to control the amount of sweat and monitor how it looks so that it remains consistent in every shot.

[MIDDLE]
In this scene, the camera tracks with Indy and Mac as they are dragged from the trunk of the car. They quickly discover that the "American" soldiers are actually Soviets in disguise, who bring them into the hangar and order Indy to find a crate that contains the remains of an alien.

[BOTTOM]
Ray Winstone and Harrison Ford. Deming, New Mexico..

[LEFT]
It was Cate's first scene when I took this and we were all excited to see her. She stepped out of the car already in character. I don't mean that she got out of the car and was mean to everyone (she was "Mean Girl" on the call sheet, although her character's name is Irina Spalko). She was delightful, of course, but as soon as she started to rehearse and the cameras started to roll, she was every inch the villain she was portraying. It was one of those times in my career when I was able to witness an actor having a lot of fun with her or his character.

[ABOVE]
This was Cate's first shot in the movie and the first posed photograph she did for me. The sun was disappearing quickly into the clouds so I had to move fast to keep the sunset in the background.

[LEFT]
One of my first posed shots of Cate on the set. She is facing the movie camera; in the background are huge sheets of silk used to diffuse the lighting and give a soft daylight effect.

[ABOVE]

This is one of my favorite images from the New Mexico location. As Steven was lining up his shot, I moved really close behind him with a wide-angle lens and caught the perfect image of him with Cate. Working with Steven on several films, I've watched the way he lines up scenes and was waiting for this moment to happen. Because I was ready, I got this frame with a single, perfectly timed shot.

[RIGHT]

We were fighting the light at the end of this shooting day. The sun was setting fast and we really had to move. There was no time to pose for stills, so I positioned myself to the left of the camera. Steven was on the right, getting Cate's eyeline set. I quickly grabbed a single frame in that moment—and it was the perfect one; after that, her hand was always a little too high for my angle. It was a treat to watch Steven and the actors work out Indy and Spalko's first scene together; they were having a lot of fun developing Cate's character.

Even if you look closely, you can't see Steven's head under this hat, but he's there. Steven is a hat man, usually baseball caps. I loved this hat on him instead–it's much more photogenic.

This is a lovely moment when Steven and Cate were silhouetted against the door. When Cate saw a print of this image, she drew a heart on it–the best approval rating I've ever received. This shot was taken at Downey Studios in Los Angeles, weeks after our trip to Deming. As you can see, the matching between the New Mexico location and the studio set is quite exact.

Cate Blanchett, Downey Studios, Los Angeles, California.

One of my favorite things to do is to step back from the action and observe the whole scene. While the scene is unfolding in front of the camera the crew is deeply involved in performing their own parts, all carefully plotted and executed.

Almost a ballet, the whip shot. Harrison saw me in front of him and instinctively went for it, knowing that the shot everyone wants is the one of Indy cracking the whip. I'd put myself in the right position to be on the receiving end (the movie camera was off to the side). We did several takes. The first two times he struck me on the wrist, fantastically close to the lens. Then he suggested, "You might want to move back a couple of feet." I think I backed up a foot. The third time, he clipped the lens hood. He managed to repeat the gesture with precision several more times, his perfect aim delivering the perfect image.

Note: While the shots in this gatefold all represent action at the beginning of the film, they were shot at the Downey Studios set.

I am truly amazed by Harrison's agility and commitment. Another actor would have used a stuntman to leap off high crates. He did every jump himself. Could I do it? Would I do it? No way. Nor would I swing down from the roof on a rope to land in the back of a moving vehicle. Every image in this sequence depicts the man himself, rather than a head replacement or a stuntman.

[LEFT & ABOVE]

Long before the cameras roll—even before many of the crew start to work on
a film—the actors are out there learning the skills they need to take on
the persona of the character they will portray. Out at the old Agua Dulce
airport near Fresno, California, Shia works with stunt crew to learn the
sword-fighting skills he will need when his character confronts Spalko later
in the film.

2

Rocket Sled & Doom Town

Deming and Las Cruces,
New Mexico; and
Hollywood soundstages

Before leaving New Mexico, we filmed two other major sequences. At the peak of the action inside Hangar 51, Indy jumps on a rocket sled and battles a scary Soviet soldier. The rocket sled shoots from the hangar at full speed, then through an opening in the wall of a bunker, and races across the landscape on rails until it is finally stopped by buffers at the end of the track.

The rocket sled was another 1950s artifact that caught George and Steven's imaginations. It was bascially a platform propelled by rockets that moves on a set of rails. They were used during the Cold War, on tracks at remote desert air bases, to test equipment that had to withstand extreme acceleration. A world land speed record (6,416 mph!) was set by a rocket sled as recently as 2003. Ours was an amazing piece of set engineering and much larger than the originals–production designer Guy Hendrix Dyas created something really impressive.

This sequence actually was shot in reverse of how it appears on film: We did the exterior shots of the rocket sled in Las Cruces first, and the early part of the fight,

[RIGHT]
Stand-in gopher. Ghost Ranch, New Mexico.

inside the hangar, on soundstages a month later. Both were challenging for getting good stills because of the high-speed action and the low lighting levels for the interior work. But, as I describe in the Introduction, I got lucky the night we were shooting outside.

Shooting stills on a soundstage is much different: You have less room to maneuver and change angles, for one thing. And you're more dependent on the lighting the film's DP has designed. Again, I was fortunate, because Steven's longtime DP, Janusz Kaminski, is a master of his craft and his creative lighting is so interesting—it's different for every movie and every scene, always a new and refreshing look. For me it was just a question of making sure that my angles brought out the best in the scene as it was lit.

If the rocket sled scenes were dark and moody, the "Doom Town" sequence was the polar opposite. After the rocket sled fight, Indy stumbles into what at first looks like an ordinary suburban subdivision, circa 1950. In fact it is a "dummy" town built by the U.S. government as an atom bomb test site. And the bomb is about to go off.

At the Deming airport, productin designer Guy Hendrix Dyas and his team built several full-scale houses, inside and out, to accommodate all kinds of shooting angles. (Much later, in the parking lot of Kerner Optical across the bay from San Francisco, a miniature of the whole town was blown to bits.) The sidewalks were peopled with perfectly costumed dummies of adults, kids, pets, and even an ice cream vendor. Everything was done in very bright, garish colors, and in the glare of the desert sun the effect

was eerie. It wasn't meant to look real for more than an instant. The typical American suburb has an iconic role in Steven's work, but this was a bizarre new take on it—and for a photographer the surreal set was a golden opportunity to get some interesting shots.

In this case, the matching interior shots for the Doom Town scenes were done on location. Indy goes inside one of the houses, looking desperately for shelter before the bomb goes off. Just in time, he crawls inside a refrigerator (period-accurate, of course). After the big blast, the fridge ends up several miles from the Doom Town set, in the desert at Las Cruces. This is where we photographed Harrison crawling out of his makeshift bomb shelter. The atmospheric, dawn-light shots of him up in the surrounding hills were the last things we did in New Mexico.

[RIGHT]

This was the first time I had shot at Downey Studios in Los Angeles. The stages are huge and the space is vast—it used to be an aircraft factory. Guy built the rocket sled lab here, where Indy fights with Dov and pushes him through a plate glass window. During the fight, a launch button is pushed and the rocket sled blasts off with Indy and Dov on board.

[FOLLOWING PAGES]

Back in Las Cruces, this is the location where the rocket sled comes to the end of its run. Indy and Dov have blacked out due to the G-forces produced by the high speed of the trip. Naturally, being the hero, Indy wakes first and makes his escape. When we did this scene, it was evening and the temperature in the desert had dropped dramatically. It was freezing and the wind was blowing up a dust storm that mixed with the smoke to create a compelling visual atmosphere.

[LEFT]

DP Janusz Kaminski at Ghost Ranch, waiting, waiting for the light. It was supposed to be a hot sunny day, but we had heavy cloud cover. I took this photograph the day before we started shooting the movie. We had just gone out to the location to shoot some tests. Luckily, Steven brought the sun with him the next day.

[ABOVE]

One of the treats of traveling with this movie circus is the chance to see new places and meet unusual people. Virgil, seen here, is one of the managers of Ghost Ranch. His family has worked on the ranch for generations. When I saw him standing by, a cowboy holding a white umbrella with the range in the background, I couldn't resist taking his picture.

[PRECEDING PAGES]

We left the hotel around 4:30 A.M. to get this image of Indy in the dawn light. The rigging crew had built steps up the side of a steep hill to help us climb to the location. I think the grips must have been there since midnight; they prepped the camera and crane in the dark to film this whole sequence.

Doom Town was funky, weird, and magical in its own way. It's a set that was built by the U.S. government to be blown away by an atom bomb test. Indy, on the run from the Soviets after the rocket sled sequence, comes across this temporary community, whose inhabitants are unnervingly silent. Before I ever saw the set built in Deming, New Mexico, Guy promised me that I would have fun there. I did, and I got some great shots as did Steven.

[LEFT & ABOVE]

The colors and plastic people were really wild. Steven could not resist getting behind the camera and shooting vignettes of the "dummy life" of a small American town.

[PRECEDING RIGHT-HAND PAGE]

Steven consults with Industrial Light & Magic (ILM) visual effects supervisor Pablo Helman on a setup in Doom Town. There was a lot of visual effects work on this set–they would have to re-create it later as a scale miniature for the atomic blast at Kerner Optical in San Rafael. A photographer can't help but have fun and shoot a lot of images when she or he is able to work on a set like this.

[ABOVE]

Working with a movie crew on location, away from family and home, your coworkers become your extended family. Steven really nurtures this family feeling because for him, family is the most important thing in life. Whenever possible, crew members' real families are made welcome too. Steven's lovely wife, Kate Capshaw, was a frequent visitor on set and was very much a friend to the whole crew (of course, Kate is an *Indy* veteran, having played Willie in *Temple of Doom*). It's rare to catch them together, but this little interlude happened while Steven was waiting for the camera to be set. I think it shows just how much in love they are. Their mutual affection makes them particularly dear to the crew.

[RIGHT]

Harrison and Steven are comfortable together without having to make small talk–it's a little like watching an old married couple.

[LEFT]

Indy realizes that the town is a bomb site and takes shelter in a refrigerator. Imagine the conditions: the temperature outside is over 100 degrees; the temperature in the kitchen is even higher with powerful movie lights; you're a tall guy and you have to fit yourself into a poorly ventilated fridge. Yes, it's really, really hot and uncomfortable.

[ABOVE]

Indy escapes from the A-bomb blast that destroyed Doom Town by hiding in a fridge. He is picked up by government men and taken to a decontamination center where he is scrubbed down and measured for radioactivity. This decontamination scene was later shot in Los Angeles, at Universal Studios. Because there were reflection problems in the glass window, the camera here is unmanned. Whenever I am on a set where there may be reflection problems, I wear black. It's not a fashion statement; it's just a practical solution. It also helps you blend into the background, reducing the element of distraction for cast and crew.

3

MARSHALL COLLEGE

New Haven and Essex,
Connecticut; soundstages;
Paramount Studios back lot

Day 9 began with a long bus ride from Deming to
El Paso, Texas, where we caught a charter flight
to Bradley, Connecticut; it ended with another
bus ride into downtown New Haven. We were following
Indy: After his adventures in the desert at the start of the
movie, he retreats to his classroom at Marshall College,
where he has long taught archaeology when he's not off on
some secret mission. But now he's in trouble with the feds,
who believe he has links to the Soviets, and he's forced to
take a sabbatical. His friend Dean Stanton (played by Jim
Broadbent) has to give him the bad news.

The production looked on the West Coast for a location
for the college, but there really was no place with buildings
that had enough age and grandeur. So they arranged to
do the filming at Yale, which was perfect. It caused a big
stir in New Haven, and incredibly detailed arrangements
had to be made to close streets, create period facades, take
precautions with old buildings—the normal location issues
in an urban environment. But it was worth it to capture the
wonderful character of the setting, which comes out in the
stills: the stonework, iron gates, paneled halls, the stately

[RIGHT]
Harrison Ford on train station platform, Essex, Connecticut.

university quad. Scenes we shot there included the Dean (Jim Broadbent) talking with Indy, a students' anti-Communist demonstration, and events at a train station where Indy and Mutt (Shia LaBeouf) meet for the first time.

Day 10 was Shia's first day on the set, and he plunged right into some major action scenes. The Russians catch up with Jones at Marshall, and there's a wild chase that begins in a diner (shot later on the Paramount Studios back lot). They race through the grounds of the college, with Indy on the back of Mutt's motorcycle. Shia had been well trained by the stunt crew, and Harrison expressed a lot of confidence in his riding–which was good, since they both did their own stunts here. As they roar through a dignified study hall (actually a university dining room, re-dressed), there's a spectacular wipeout where they and the bike slide under a desk … but they get back on and keep going. My shots of this are retouched so they don't reveal the wires that kept Harrison and Shia safe while they jumped off and on the bike. These wires were of course, removed by Lucasfilm's Industrial Light & Magic (ILM) in the final composition as well.

This was a difficult scene to shoot, even when I planned my shots out in advance. For a scene where Indy is riding in a car, I mounted a camera on a crane arm to shoot through the window. But sometimes during a take, the camera movement would change and I would get nothing, or just the tops of heads. My camera would simply end up in the wrong place, especially when the movie camera got in close to the actors. I tried to work around these obstacles by joining the film camera crew. Nothing

beats being on the camera car in the right position–even if that means lying down and contorting yourself into a position that's hard on your back. With luck there will be a moment when the camera pulls back a little so you can get the shot. Once again luck was on my side here.

Some of the last shots we did in Connecticut were at the train station at Essex, where Indy boards a train heading out of town. This is where Mutt tracks him down. Essex is on a commuter line, and it has a railway museum with old steam engines and carriages. The production brought in 1950s autos to reinforce the period atmosphere.

Back in California, we rounded out the Marshall scenes with shots of Arnie's Diner (named after Steven's father) on the Paramount Studios back lot–both the diner interior and its alley entrance. In dressing this street set, production designer Guy Hendrix Dyas also created a hat shop whose signage said "David James Hatter" as a nod to me, for which I'm grateful. And on a soundstage at Universal, Guy and his set decorators created an interior for Indy's home that's like an Indiana Jones museum, full of artifacts and memorabilia. I know they had fun doing it, and Harrison enjoyed inhabiting it. He was always anxious, he said, that any place associated with his character should live up to expectations. This is where Mutt shows Indy a letter from his guardian Harold Oxley (John Hurt); and where the professor listens to the advice of his friend Stanton, consults his library, and then packs his Indy gear for the next stage of the adventure.

On the first day of shooting in Connecticut, our circus set up at Yale University. We had left behind the dust and heat for a lush green park in the middle of New Haven. It was heaven by comparison. I had never been to Yale before and was astounded to see the architectural similarities between the campus buildings and some of the great English universities such as Oxford and Cambridge. We started our shoot in Dr. Jones's classroom [ABOVE]. Jim Broadbent, a very accomplished actor from my U.K. homeland and an old friend, joined us for these scenes.

[RIGHT]

Thank you, Janusz, for this shot! We were working on a scene in the corridor outside Dr. Jones's classroom and a single shaft of light was coming through the window from outside. Janusz called me over to see. I sent for Indy's hat and … voila!

It was a wet day, but the crew was still more than happy to be away from dust, wind, and searing heat of the New Mexico desert. We shot at the Essex railway station. This scene is where Indy and Mutt (Shia LaBeouf) meet for the first time.

On the bike with his cap and leather jacket, Shia bore a distinct resemblance to Marlon Brando in *The Wild One.*

[ABOVE]
Steven's thinking aloud!

[RIGHT]
Steven needed a close shot of Mutt looking for Indy on the moving train. A special compact vehicle was used with the camera mounted on a mini-crane and operated remotely. This gave the operator freedom to be high or low. The vehicle was small enough not only to carry the equipment but also to move along the platform without harming the extras.

[LEFT]

No, it's not a face-off between Shia with a knife and Steven with his
iPhone! There was going to be a scene in the film that we shot much later,
where Shia has to throw his knife with incredible accuracy, so he had
to practice all the time in anticipation of that moment. And the iPhone
was very new at the time, so Steven was always busy practicing as well.
Watching Steven and Shia together [ABOVE] is like watching a good
relationship between a father and son–again, it's that whole family feeling
that develops during Steven's productions.

[ABOVE]

When I first saw this shop façade on the set at Paramount Studios in Los Angeles, I thought, "Are they trying to tell me that I'm a bit of a mad hatter? That maybe I'm in the wrong game?" Seriously, though, this gesture really touched me. Thank you, Guy. My dad always wanted me to be in movies.

[LEFT]

Here, Steven is setting up a camera angle for the scene where Mutt rides along the platform next to the moving train. I had to shoot with a really wide-angle lens to get as much open space as possible in the frame. Maneuvering room was very limited and shooting with a longer lens would have crowded the frame with people.

This is one of the mysteries of filmmaking: You
shoot a motorcycle chase sequence on location
(the bottom photo was shot outside Yale College
in Connecticut), and then weeks later you are
on the back lot at Paramount Studios where
you shoot the scene that leads up to the chase
through the streets of New Haven. It's a script
supervisor's nightmare to make sure everything
matches up, but it usually does.

Don't try this at home—the actor was able to get his close-up while maneuvering at high speed through a crowd of people. Most of the crowd
was made up of stunt people who knew when to get out of the way.

[LEFT & ABOVE]

The choice of angle and lens on these shots was, first and foremost, for impact. I wanted to separate the action from the background and, just as importantly, a long lens (300mm) kept me away from the charging car. It was much safer that way. Gary Powell, our stunt chief, put a man in charge of watching out for me and he had one hand on my belt ready to drag me away in the event that the driver of the vehicle lost control.

[ABOVE]
Shia LaBeouf and Harrison Ford on Mutt's motorcycle. New Haven, Connecticut.

[LEFT]
Statue of Marcus Brody. New Haven, Connecticut.

Our heroes come to rest at the feet of a student who, ignoring all the excitement, takes the opportunity to ask a routine question about archaeology of Professor Jones. The student was played by a young actor whom we will undoubtedly see more of in the future—Chet Hanks, Tom Hanks's son.

Steven belongs to the camera. He is always very hands on and loves to get on the wheels, which, of course, I love. This is the type of image that is always published. Either that or the pose where he is framing the scene with his hands.

4

GATEWAY TO THE AMAZON

Universal soundstages and back lot

At this point in the movie, the setting gets exotic, as you'd expect in an *Indy* film. Mutt has enlisted Professor Jones to help find his mother, who is Indy's old flame, Marion Ravenwood (Karen Allen). She's been kidnapped by the Soviets, along with Mutt's father-figure, Harold Oxley, because Oxley knows (among other things) where to find the ancient Lost City of Akator in Peru.

Akator is where all the plot threads converge: a mysterious ancient culture, Spanish conquistadors, a visit by aliens—and a crystal skull with psychic powers that Oxley found in an eerie cemetery. The backstory on the Soviets' interest is that Stalin had been and the KGB still are obsessed with a legend about the crystal skull; they believe that whoever controls the paranormal will gain an edge in world domination and that the skull promises access to otherworldly power. Spalko, Cate's character, runs their psychic research program, and she wants the skull badly.

[RIGHT]
Harrison Ford. Universal Studios, Los Angeles, California.

So Indy and Mutt wind up in a rough frontier town on the edge of the Amazon jungle, looking for Oxley and Marion. They get word that Oxley is being held prisoner nearby, in a sanitarium run by nuns. The Peruvian village, dubbed Nazca Town, was created by re-dressing an existing street on the Universal Studios back lot, normally part of the studio tour. (Many of the South American scenes were done on soundstages and studio lots.) Its centerpiece was a market area, and the whole thing looked incredibly real–the art department brought in textiles and other Peruvian items, a llama and other South American beasts, and put a layer of age on everything. The atmosphere was so authentic it really felt as though you were on location in Peru. I probably shot way more than was needed, but I had a lot of fun on the set.

When Mutt and Indy find the sanitarium–the interior was entirely built on a soundstage, complete with real cockroaches–Oxley is gone but has left cryptic messages scrawled on a wall. These clues lead our heroes to a crumbling

cemetery, where they find the crystal skull in a Spanish conquistador's tomb. Oxley, taking orders from the skull, had tried to restore it to the Lost City, but couldn't find a way in, so he hid it in the grave.

The cemetery, built on Stage 27 at Universal, was a classic *Indiana Jones* set, with intricate underground tunnels, vaults, scorpions, and, of course, deadly surprises. At the end of shooting there, Steven called the crew together and paid Guy Hendrix Dyas a huge compliment, saying that in all his career he had never been given such an exciting set to shoot on. It was an exciting place for all of us to work, and DP Janusz Kaminski made it even more so with his distinctive lighting–adding to the mood, mystery, and the tension of the scenes we shot there.

As they explore, Indy and Mutt are attacked by a couple of Nazca warriors and have to fight their way through. Our heroes don't get far, though. Spalko's Soviet commandos recapture them after they emerge from the cemetery and take them off to a remote jungle camp.

[PREVIOUS LEFT-HAND PAGE]
Harrison Ford and Shia LaBeouf. Fresno, California.

[PREVIOUS RIGHT-HAND PAGE]
Harrison Ford and Shia LaBeouf. Universal Studios back lot, Los Angeles, California.

[LEFT]
On their quest to find Professor Oxley, Indy and Mutt arrive in a Peruvian village. The village, conveniently situated on the back lot at Universal Studios in Burbank, California, was a delight to photograph. The art directors and set dressers had done such a wonderful job putting this location together, it felt as though you were really on site in South America. Casting rounded up local extras who looked like they could have been flown in directly from Peru.

[RIGHT]
The nun in the picture is our lovely script lady, Anna Maria Quintana, a regular member of Steven's on-set family.

[BOTTOM]
Harrison Ford and Shia LaBeouf. Universal Studios back lot, Los Angeles, California.

[ABOVE]

Steven was looking for the ideal angle for the camera to sweep the wall. This shot was a must for me. I love watching Steven work out shots; you can sense the creative process at work in his mind and see it manifest in his actions.

[RIGHT]

The light was perfect for this shot of George in front of Oxley's wall of clue-filled scrawls. I rarely had to ask George to pose for shots; he just feels the camera when it's on him and gives you the picture you want without any fuss.

[LEFT]

Smoke, shafts of light, and a hand reaching through cell bars toward the camera—the perfect ingredients for a photo. It had to be black and white of course, which is still my favorite medium.

[ABOVE]
On-the-set hairspray for Shia LeBeouf. Unverisal Studios soundstage, Los Angeles, California.

[RIGHT]
Following Oxley's clues, Indy and Mutt arrive at the Nazca cemetery. This was an amazing set, full of nooks and crannies, spider webs, dust, and mysteries. When we had completed several days of shooting on this set, Steven called the crew together and congratulated Guy, as he put it, on having designed "the most interesting and creative set" he had ever shot on. I think the whole crew felt the same way; it really was quite extraordinary.

[FOLLOWING PAGES]
Janusz made the lighting very low in this scene, to create the right mood for the cemetery at night. I had to push the limits to get this shot of Mutt being attacked by the skeleton guard. [LEFT-HAND PAGE] The image is a bit blurry, capturing the speed and surprise of the moment. The action took place in just a split second, and then the guard disappeared down a well.

[ABOVE]
Normally, I keep out of the actor's line of sight in scenes like this. Otherwise, it's hard for them to feel like they're on their own. I thought I had found a spot where I wouldn't be a distraction, but the action changed and I was left with Shia looking straight into my lens. I had no way out, so I just kept on shooting without making eye contact.

[RIGHT]
Another day at Downey Studios and another day in the catacombs. I had a real treasure trove of sets to shoot on. There was a great feeling of being in a real place here–it was quite creepy, but with a few laughs thrown in. I don't think Shia was overly keen on having to handle a mummified corpse at close range, even if it was a prop. A great attention to detail had gone into making these mummies and they looked very spooky. In this scene Indy finds a crystal skull, which was shrouded in mystery until the film's release. This secrecy was well-protected, even amongst the crew. The set was put into lockdown when propmaster Doug Harlocker brought the skull out for the shots it was needed for, and then it was put quickly under wraps again.

I loved the lighting in this set—the interior of Spalko's tent, which was set up at Sony Studios in Los Angeles, where we would later shoot the Soviet's camp and some of the Temple of Akator scenes. Janusz used a lot of white globes and cast the light through silks to achieve a soft look. Spalko is interrogating Indy about the crystal skull so Harrison couldn't move a lot. He was locked into that chair for hours, immobilized, although he does manage to punch Mac in the nose (as promised). When I first saw the set, I thought it was going to be tough to get in there, but it was actually fairly easy. Janusz's lighting setup made it comfortable for me to shoot from my own angles away from the movie camera.

[RIGHT]
Cate is a chameleon. With any character she plays, she becomes that person. One totally forgets that it's Cate behind the costume and makeup. I love photographing her; she intuitively picks up on what photographers are after and brings a lot to each session beyond just being a subject. In every shoot we did, she would make suggestions that were constructive and really helped make the most of every photograph. Any chance I have to shoot with her again, I'll be there. This shot was taken during a gallery shoot I did of all the actors in costume at Downey Studios.

[LEFT]
Harrison Ford and Ray Winstone. Sony Studios, Los Angeles, California.

[RIGHT]

Video Village (at Sony Studios, where we shot Spalko's camp)—that's what we called the monitor area where Steven, DP Janusz, script supervisor Ana Maria, and producer Frank Marshall watched takes with critical eyes. In this shot, Igor (who plays Dov), Cate, Steven, Frank, Harrison, and Ana Maria review a take.

[LEFT]

Spalko tries to get information out of Mutt, who stands his ground. Yes, it was very hot right by that fire. The flames were not on camera, but they made for a good lighting effect.

[BELOW]

This was a very difficult shot. Oxley (John Hurt) had a complicated speech to make while he wrote in an ancient Mayan script. Two cameras were used on this shot so that the expert on Mayan scripts who had his hand under John's arm to guide its movements could be hidden in the final shot.

[LEFT]

Mutt's mum, Marion Ravenwood from *Raiders of the Lost Ark* (Karen Allen), makes her first screen appearance in the movie. Karen was stunning and delivered her trademark smile. This is one of those moments when it was important to be right where the movie camera lens was to get every aspect right.

[BELOW & RIGHT]

Indy hates snakes, but in this case a snake was the only thing available to fish him out of a deadly sand pit. The pit was, of course, fake. A huge hole in the floor was filled with sand and the bottom of the pit had a movable floor that could be raised or lowered to send Harrison up or down. The snake, though, was very real (though in some shots a duplicate snake made by Stan Winston Studio was used).

5

JUNGLE CHASE

Hawaii; Sony Studios sound-stages

O ur last location work for *Crystal Skull* involved shooting action scenes of capture, escape, chase, and recapture in the Amazon jungle. For the jungle setting, our team discovered a 16,000-acre private property on the tropical east coast of Hawaii's Big Island—the Shipman Estate—with the right kind of vegetation and a mile-long road through the forest that was perfect for the chase sequences. The owners even granted us permission to cut some new trails so we could run vehicles back and forth. Days 13 and 14 of the shoot were pack-and-travel days for me: from Connecticut back to Los Angeles, then loading my gear onto a charter flight for Hawaii. Day 15 was devoted to setup and prep.

On Day 16 (July 11, 2007), the cameras rolled again. Karen Allen (Marion) and John Hurt (Oxley) joined cast and crew on the set for the first time, and their presence deepened the sense of *Indiana Jones* history being made. A Hawaiian *kahu* (guardian or minister) gave a blessing to the production, sprinkling sanctified salt water and praying for our good fortune. Then we started in, getting shots of the convoy that's taking Indy, his friends, and the Soviet bad guys deep into the jungle to find the Lost City of Akator. This was a difficult setting to shoot, very hot and very humid, with narrow windy roads.

[RIGHT]
John Hurt and Cate Blanchett. Hawaii.

True to the series tradition of narrow escapes and hair-raising chases, a lot of action is packed into this part of the movie (again, some of it shot later on soundstages). After being captured, Indy and Mutt are reunited with Marion and Oxley at the jungle camp. Mutt leads them on a failed escape in which Indy and Marion are caught in a sand pit, and he pulls them out with a snake–Indy's least favorite animal. Meanwhile, thinking they were done for, Marion has told Indy that he's really Mutt's father! Of course they're recaptured and the journey resumes–with lots more adventures before they reach Akator, including a gun battle among speeding vehicles, an attack by giant red ants (done in CGI, so I framed my images to exclude the ants), and a full-blown sword duel between Mutt and Spalko. There were wonderful chances for me to capture the action in stills: combatants leaping from one vehicle to another, Cate/Spalko dueling with Shia/Mutt (both of them had extensive sword fighting training), Indy punching out Mac after Mac betrays him yet again.

Hawaii presented some new challenges, too. The humid air was hazardous to camera gear, which had to be thoroughly cleaned after each day. For travel, the film camera crew helped out; they packed my boxes with silica gel to absorb the moisture. My biggest puzzle was how to get my camera close enough to the action and keep it stable. Again, the grip crew came through, making special brackets so that I could mount my camera next to the film camera. Then I could travel on the vehicle, watch the action, and press the remote at the right moment. Even so, it was impossible at times to take a shot–for example, if the camera was in too close, it would be shooting over the actors because of parallax. In those situations, Steven would allow me to "re-stage" the moment while we were stopped for a reload or lens change. Later, back on the computer, I would work on the images, blurring the backgrounds to simulate movement.

Being on location provides many chances for behind-the-scenes pictures–of the crew working or talent relaxing–and I took advantage of breaks in the action to record off-camera moments. George was on hand for a while in Hawaii–the place where he and Steven first got together decades ago. The crew gave Cate a big black umbrella to shield her from sun and rain; I love the umbrella shots. On July 13, Harrison celebrated a birthday with a big cake on set. And a few days before we wrapped in Hawaii, Harrison and I stopped by a local school where the kids had hung a big welcome banner they'd made for the movie production. We took a picture in front of the banner to send to the kids.

On July 17, Tropical Storm Cosme was upgraded to a hurricane and seemed to be heading for the islands. We were going to shoot a waterfall for later bluescreen work, but the weather put an end to that idea: the main storm missed us, but delivered buckets of rain. On Friday, July 20–Day 24 of the shoot–we packed up and flew back to L.A. that weekend.

[ABOVE]
This is not just a shot of Guy Hendrix Dyas in a jungle; it's a shot of him in the jungle he and his team built! We didn't plan this shot, but he was definitely wearing the right color shirt to stand out from all that green.

[LEFT]
Auli'i Mitchell, the Kumuhula, gives the production a blessing on the first day of shooting on the Big Island of Hawaii.

[LEFT & ABOVE]
Janusz was using a large silk to light Harrison in this scene. As I mentioned before, I love silhouettes and couldn't resist taking this shot. It worked particularly well, I think, as I was also able to photograph Harrison's reflection in the mirror too.

[TOP]
Cate behind a gun.

[MIDDLE]
Shooting in the jungle produces all sorts of problems: conditions are extremely variable–vastly different from the controlled environment of the studio; there's humidity; high contrast when the sun shines; heavy rain; and several constantly moving vehicles that need to be tracked. I think that 99 percent of everything we shot in the jungle was on dollying vehicles. It was very difficult to steady a camera with a long lens while seated on a vehicle that was racing along a jungle track, bumping over palm fronds and potholes. The way I got around this obstacle was to mount my camera on the crane arm, which was counter-balanced, and therefore a lot smoother. This worked most of the time, except when the camera was too close to the actors, or when it got close to the ground or other obstructions that could bump it.

[BOTTOM]
Executive producer Kathy Kennedy is one of the keenest and most enthusiastic photographers I know. It was nice to catch her in front of the lens for a change, talking with Cate in a rare quiet moment. Cate used the umbrella to protect her makeup from the weather and to keep her from being sunburned.

[RIGHT]
Steven Spielberg talks to Cate Blanchett while John Hurt and Ray Winstone look on. To Spielberg's left is first assistant director Adam Somner. Hawaii.

Well, it can't all be serious work. There has to be a moment for a laugh and if Steven can find it, I promise you, he won't let it pass. At this moment, he was showing a stand-in where to be behind the wheel in order to be kicked in the right place.

A very effective way to deal with the high contrast light situation in the jungle is to use smoke. Special effects crews would go ahead of the camera and smoke up the jungle for each take. If the wind was up it would take a few runs to get it right.

Stunt co-coordinator Gary Powell shows Steven a setup before we go on the road. Doing stunts in fast-moving vehicles is dangerous at best, so no expense is ever spared to make sure our actors and crew are safe. The stunt team designs the fights and rehearses the actors in every move, coordinating with specialist wire people to secure the cast in the vehicles.

[LEFT]

There I was with everything in one shot at Downey Studios–bluescreen, actors, cameras, and crew. When I'm working as a unit photographer, I'm always looking for a shot that gives a sense of the scale of the project I'm shooting. This is a good example that characterizes the scope of the *IJ4* production.

[PRECEDING PAGES]

I have the best job in the world. I get to photograph lovely people all day long. Cate is one of the best subjects to photograph; no two shots are ever quite the same with her.

[ABOVE]

These were shots that I had to set up with the help of the camera crew. The film camera was in so tight, I would only have gotten the tops of the actors' heads. To avoid this, I climbed onto the back of the jeep and had the crew run the motion slower for me, using a shutter speed that gave me the action I needed.

[RIGHT]

Silhouettes–I love them, always have. I manage to get a few on every movie I do. In this case at Downey I had to time the moment just right to photograph the swords in the proper place, which wasn't easy considering the speed at which they were moving. On the other hand, I shot from a distance, giving myself more room to concentrate–I wasn't so close that I had to duck.

[ABOVE]
Harrison Ford and gaffer David Devlin. Hawaii.

[RIGHT]
At the Universal lot, I was shooting from behind the silk sheet when my daughter Chia (who was working for the film's publicist, Deb Wuliger) called for me to come around to the other side. I was reluctant at first because I really wanted to take another shot, but she became so insistent I had to comply. She was right. I managed to grab this image just before we wrapped. Thank you, Chia; you have a great eye.

6

THE LOST TEMPLE OF AKATOR

Downey, Universal, Sony, Warner Bros. soundstages and exterior lots

Completing *Crystal Skull* on schedule, with the bar of excellence set so high, called on all the filmmakers' talent and ingenuity—and, in the end, on just about every movie-making space available in greater Los Angeles. Throughout August and September 2007, the production used several different studios to film what couldn't be done on location. Often we needed huge stages or back lots to accommodate the scope of the action or the enormous physical sets. At Universal's Freeway Park and Falls Lake, for example, scenes were shot of Indy's gang heading over a waterfall in a boat.

Because we were coming up to the film's climax, there naturally had to be a whole array of formidable obstacles that Indy must overcome before he can penetrate the heart of the Lost City. First there's a giant obelisk, carved with hieroglyphs, which Indy and company must somehow raise into place to unlock the temple entrance. They solve this riddle using simple yet ingenious leverage techniques like those that the ancient builders used to build huge structures without modern tools. As always, a physical set was preferred to visual effects (VFX), so the practical effects crew devised a real stone obelisk. After our heroes get past this, they're trapped on a trick staircase that spirals down into the temple, with 20-foot stone treads that are

quickly retracting, forcing them to leap for their lives. Steven got very excited when production designer Guy Hendrix Dyas sketched this out for him, and the crew built a fully working system on the biggest soundstage at Sony Studios. I took shots of the obelisk on stage, and of the stair set from above, showing the actors on wires, but since visual effects and stunt work were involved, it was impossible to show all the action in stills.

For pure artistry, nothing could top the sets for the final scenes, which take place in the heart of Akator Temple. There was another giant stairway, which barely fit inside Stage 16, the largest on the Warner Bros. lot. There was an elaborate antechamber, replete with ancient artifacts from many cultures–Egyptian, Etruscan, Mesopotamian. From that chamber, Indy's contingent must pass through a final doorway. In another triumph of practical engineering (and using the psychic power of the crystal skull, as the story has it), the door cracks open when Indy places the skull in it. Seeing Harrison set off the opening mechanism for the first time was a highlight for everyone on the crew.

One day near the end of the L.A. shooting marathon stands out. On September 25 (Day 67 of the 80-day shoot), cast and crew gathered on Stage 16 to film the heroes as they enter the heart of the temple: a vast round chamber with thirteen thrones around the perimeter. Seated in each is an intricate crystal skeleton created by John Rosengrant's props team at Stan Winston Studio. They are the remains of aliens from another dimension, who built the Lost City millennia ago. One is missing its skull. (In the backstory, the Nazca legend grew out of this alien

visitation; and these thirteen visitors were trapped in Akator because conquistadors stole the crystal skull.) As the cameras rolled, Oxley edged toward the headless skeleton with the skull. Spalko grabs it, but it's pulled from her hands onto the alien (a CGI effect). This of course triggers a massive dimensional shift that destroys Akator, the Soviets–everything but our heroes.

Needless to say, the excitement and secrecy around this part of the shoot were off the charts. Steven, as usual, arrived on the set before everyone else to map out his shots. A bit later, George Lucas showed up, sitting beside Steven and weighing in on various takes. Series producers Frank Marshall and Kathy Kennedy also were on hand. The extra personnel and tight quarters on these stages made my work harder than usual, but the rewards were great. I was able to get up close and personal to those astounding skeletons. Guy's brilliantly colored and detailed set pieces glowed under DP Janusz Kaminski's dramatic lighting. And the lights caught every shifting expression on the actors' faces: Oxley's astonished wonder, Spalko's focused fierceness, and the terror, bravery, and affection that united Indy, Marion, and Mutt at the story's climax.

There would be more scenes to pick up, more bluescreen work, and eventually hundreds of shots to be composited at ILM for the final film. But the essence of *Indiana Jones and the Kingdom of the Crystal Skull* was there in my viewfinder on this set. It's what movie viewers will see just before the temple begins to spin and disintegrate, returning the aliens to their own dimension.

[LEFT]
This was a spectacular set at Falls Lake, on the Universal Studios back lot. Because there was so much moisture, every effort had to be made to keep the lenses dry. So the cameras were covered in plastic, while the actors got wet. Just another day at the office.

135

[ABOVE & CENTER]
You might think that bluescreen work is pretty boring for a photographer to cover, but that's actually not the case. It's always a strange but intriguing thing to behold—actors behaving as if there is a set all around them (personally, I don't know how they do it). I've shot a lot of scenes on bluescreen, and they always reward me with interesting images that showcase this mysterious talent that actors have.

[ABOVE]
We needed a shot of Cate descending a cliff wall, so we built one at Downey Studios. Here, the camera tracks down with her. The background would be added later.

[LEFT & ABOVE]

How do you put a bunch of actors in a Duck vehicle and send them over a very high water-fall? You don't. You go to Falls Lake at Universal Studios, put them in the Duck and send it down a ramp. Sure, they get wet, but you can find them again afterward. And you can do it again, and again, and again.

[RIGHT]

Escaping from the temple, our actors had to run through a waterfall–again, and again, and again. I just got wet feet; they were soaked.

[PRECEDING PAGES]
The temple warriors blended into the background perfectly in these scenes, giving the whole setting a near-documentary quality. It almost felt as if I was doing a shoot for *National Geographic*. This shot on the right was a painful one for Ray Winstone (Mac). A split second after the shutter closed, he made a bad landing and sprained his ankle. With true commitment, he carried on as if nothing had happened for the remainder of the scene.

[LEFT]
These actors sat patiently for hours and hours while makeup and hair teams worked to transform them into temple guards. The process would start around 4:00 A.M. I was never there at the very start. Arriving at 6:00 A.M. was early enough for me.

[LEFT & RIGHT]
So what makes the modern day warrior go? Ice lollies and coffee, of course; just like anyone else on a hot day or on the job.

[ABOVE]

This was a rare moment on the set. Both producers Kathy Kennedy and Frank Marshall were together in the same place and weren't surrounded by people demanding answers to countless questions.

[LEFT]

Whenever I'm on the set of a film that uses bluescreen, I see it as an opportunity to get great behind-the-scenes images.

The hidden temple is located in the middle of the Amazon jungle. It was hard to re-create this on the back lot at Universal with the 101 freeway just yards away. The solution was to use a bluescreen and to fill in the backgrounds in post-production. ILM sent a crew to shoot the background imagery in South America and then stitched everything together digitally for the final film. I would love to have gone of course but we were still shooting other scenes.

[RIGHT]

The *IJ4* Bible—Steven's copy of the script. Believe me, he wasn't far away.

[ABOVE]
Steven and production designer Guy Hendrix Dyas stand in thigh-deep water at the bottom of the temple tower at Sony Studios.

[LEFT]
When I saw our stunt crew's contingent of wire riggers sitting atop the well overlooking the temple floor, it instantly called to mind the famous photo, *Construction Workers Take a Lunch Break on a Steel Beam Atop the RCA Building at Rockefeller Center* (1932) by Charles Ebbets.

[ABOVE]
Known as The Stand-By Painter, although really an accomplished artist, Tony Leonardi had to turn his careful hand to many parts on a set at Downey, making sure that everything from eliminating flares for the camera to creating and maintaining works of art was taken care of. Here he is touching up a masterpiece done in the style of Mayan frescoes.

[PRECEDING LEFT-HAND PAGE]
Steven sets an angle with Harrison holding the skull, which is the key to opening the door to the inner sanctum. This door, engineered at the Warner Bros. Studios, was a practical masterpiece of set design and construction, housing an intricate group of moving parts.

[PRECEDING RIGHT-HAND PAGE: BOTTOM]
In this scene, the film camera tracks across the faces of the group. I wanted to get a shot from a different angle. That meant holding the group for me and repositioning them. Steven gave me the time and stepped in to direct the actors for this shot of mine.

[LEFT]
This set was also Cate's last scene. It was so unusual to see Spalko letting her guard down but it was understandable in this case—the set was extremely hot because it was enclosed and because a lot of light had to be poured in due to the predominating red color (red absorbs a lot of light).

[LEFT & RIGHT]
Here we are in the interior of the Crystal Skull Room in Akator Temple. Our heroes are about to return the crystal skull to its proper place when Spalko and what is left of her Soviet soldiers surprise them. In her quest for "all knowledge," she takes the skull herself, only to prove, once again, that good prevails over evil. This was a difficult set to shoot and I had to do a lot of climbing to get the high angles. Steven set up the shot on the right for me while I balanced on the top of a stepladder.

[LEFT]
The temple is about to self-destruct and Mac is being carried away with it. Ray is on wires, of course, which I removed digitally so that one can see more of what's going on.

[TOP RIGHT]
The camera is covered with plastic here to protect it from the wind and dust that built up as the shot progressed.

[RIGHT]
In this frame, Steven is lining up a shot with camera operator Mitch Dubin. I took this photograph near the end of the shoot when everyone was feeling a little more relaxed on the set.

7

A FAMILY AFFAIR

Fresno–Yosemite International Airport; Eagle Field, near Firebaugh, California

T he final days of an epic shoot are a matter of assembling the missing pieces of a giant jigsaw puzzle. In the case of *Crystal Skull*, there was an expedition to California's Central Valley, where small, dusty airfields stood in for airports at various locations touched upon in the story: the East Coast, Mexico City, and Peru. Finally, there was the wedding of Indy and Marion, possibly the episode kept under deepest cover in this top-secret production.

The wrap day on any film is always a glorious and bittersweet time, and on *Crystal Skull* it was as if we had two wraps. The first was the day we shot the wedding scene—the last day for many of the actors and crew, including Karen Allen. The day culminated in a champagne toast to the entire cast and crew, accompanied by lots of heartfelt thank-yous from Steven, George Lucas, Frank Marshall, and Kathy Kennedy.

[RIGHT]
Shia LaBeouf, Karen Allen, Harrison Ford as Mutt picks up a stray fedora. San Fernando Valley, California.

130

Early the next morning, a reduced crew flew by charter from Los Angeles to Fresno to shoot the two airport locations. At the end of that day, there was a different kind of wrap party on the set with beer and hot dogs, and Harrison bestowing the iconic Indy fedora on Shia. We then drove nearly two hours to a second airfield, which had a fabulous World War II flight museum on site. This was the location for the final shot, where Indy and Mutt (and the motorcycle) arrive in Peru after their flight from North America. My picture of them in front of the "Aeropuerto de Nazca" shows them standing on either side of the bike with the crate lying in pieces on the ground.

It was an exhilarating but also a very emotional day, because the tiredness that we'd never had time for earlier in the production finally caught up with us. Even though this shoot, unlike the previous *Indy* films, had used only U.S. locations, it truly felt as though we had crisscrossed the globe, like one of those old planes tracing a red trail in an *Indiana Jones* travel montage. When those of us still left—Steven, George, Harrison, Shia, and

remaining crew—said our fond farewells, it was as if a family was parting after a long reunion. "Sad," said Steven "that it's been eighteen years because I should, by this time, have been shooting *Indy VII*—although it was worth waiting for the great script from David Koepp. I will miss my shooting 'family' and hope it won't be another eighteen years."

We had shared an incredible journey, and now it was time to go our separate ways. Until the next time . . .

[ABOVE, LEFT, & RIGHT]
This was a precious and much-anticipated day. All during the shoot, we had been referring to this scene as, "The Town Hall Meeting." It's Indy and Marion's wedding day. Marion, the glowing bride, and Indy, minus the whip, tie the knot. Mutt already wants to try on the hat, whip, and satchel.

In many ways, it was a day of celebration but also sadness, as a lot of the cast and crew said goodbye after the wedding scene. As we started, so we ended, with champagne and kind words from our leader. Early the next day, a reduced crew flew out before dawn to Fresno for the last day of our journey together.

It's all over—eighty days of shooting mixed in with quite a bit of travel. Everyone was emotional, happy with what had been accomplished yet sad to be saying goodbye to each other. We really did become like a family.

[LEFT & RIGHT]
The greatest gift: Harrison gave Shia one of his beloved Indy fedoras, inscribing on the inside band the message "It's all yours." Afterward, Shia told me that his two most treasured possessions are first, his mother, and second, this hat.

[MIDDLE]
Harrison Ford, Kathleen Kennedy, Steven Spielberg. Fresno, California.

[BOTTOM]
Steven Spielberg with associate producer Kristie Macosko. Fresno, California.

[PRECEDING PAGES]
Harrison Ford and Shia LaBeouf. Fresno, California.

COLOPHON

INSIGHT EDITIONS
Publisher & Creative Director: *Raoul Goff*
Art Director: *Iain R. Morris*
Acquiring Editor: *Jake Gerli*
Project Editor: *Diana Landau*
Consulting Editor: *Peter Beren*
Designers: *Jennifer Durrant & Iain R. Morris*
Production Manager: *Lina S. Palma-Temeña*
Design Production Coordinator: *Donna Lee*

Special thanks to Christopher Maas and Gabe Ely.

LUCASFILM
Executive Editor: *J. W. Rinzler*
Art Director: *Troy Alders*
Director of Publishing: *Carol Roeder*

At Lucasfilm: *A huge thanks to Tina Mills and Stacey Leong.*
At Amblin Entertainment: *Grateful thanks to Kristie Macosko, Samantha Becker, and Laurent Bouzereau—and of course to Steven Spielberg. And many, many thanks to Harrison Ford for his foreword.*

I would like to offer my personal thanks to the wonderful cast and crew, and to Steven, George, Kathy, and Frank. This book is a result of all of our work and our time together.

A special thanks to my wife, Dian, who fastidiously kept the daily log for me and kept me organized. Also a special thank you to my other daughter Deya who handled all the other distractions of life to keep my mind clear and focused.

—*David James*